6 billiOn PriMates haVing the

SaMe halluCination TogeTher

a painting

I0480271

by Wolf Larsen

ABOUT WOLF LARSEN

Wolf Larsen is an adventurer, writer, and poet who traveled through 45 countries in Latin America, Europe, the Middle East, and Asia. Wolf has lived in Chicago, Wisconsin, New York City, Honduras, Brazil, Peru, and India. He worked for nearly twelve years as a seasonal laborer in Alaska. His fiction and poetry has been published in literary magazines around the world.

Other Books by Wolf Larsen

Capitalism Sucks (non-fiction)

Pricks, Cunts, & Motherfuckers: The Novel About New York City

Eulogy for the Human Race (poems)

Three Dudes Having a Beer (a book of plays)

Ten Thousand Penises in Your Ear (a novel)

Most of Wolf Larsen's books can be purchased at Amazon.com

6 **b**i**ll**i**O**n PriM**a**t**e**s ha**V**i**ng** **t**he *S*aM**e**

*h*a**ll**u**C**i**n**a**t**i**o**n To*g**e**Th**e**r

a painting

by Wolf Larsen

I'm standing in front of a large white canvas.

The canvas – the big white canvas menacing

me with its emptiness – just becomes wider &

wider as it stands menacingly in front of me...

I take one look back at the world around me,

and then I walk straight into the empty

canvas.

And now, the reader & I are sitting together in

the immensity of this white canvas. You & I sit

on opposite sides of this white whiteness. This huge whiteness goes on for centuries & centuries! Then you & I staaaare at each other until our own bodies crumble into fish & amphibians & amoebas...

That's when half the IMMENSITY of the canvas becomes dark with words. The other half of the canvas becomes *bright* with the IMMENSITY of *color*. The color & words begin *oozing* all over each other as the forces of nature take over our brains...

That's when we plunge our hands into our testicles and pull out centuries of bliss. And then we paint the centuries of bliss all over the foreheads of adolescent "children". We reach into the centuries of our ancestors and we pull out the images that flow like sunlight...

We run together for miles & miles inside the canvas until we find ourselves in thousands of telephone calls. And all the great painters of all times – those that were famous and those who died without fame – are all surrounding us at this moment – together they're creating the largest painting that the universe has ever known!

You & I stand together and watch all the great painters create an immensity surrounding us – this immensity of the canvas surrounding us on all sides like eternal nightmares & dreams... And all these eternal nightmares & dreams are building on top of each other into the mushroom clouds of bliss soon to embrace the human race...

Suddenly, gravity disappears and you & I begin

rising spontaneously in the air... Except, we're

not rising in the air, we're rising into the

et*e*Rna*l* *u*P-*eve*rY*thi***n**g of the painting... And

the painting is SWALLOWING all the words in

our heads...

The human race – the entire human race –

looks up in TERROR as the painting *rises* above

the world and SWALLOWS the heavens and

SWALLOWS the stars and SWALLOWS the

sun...

I am standing by your side. And you watch

petrified as I begin sp*l*itT*i*ng-U*p*-intO-pieCe*s*

and suddenly color & paint & words of poetry

are all flying out of me, and now all the color &

paint & words are marching around you in

circles of craziness threatening to devour you with all my insanity...

Then the painting launches you & all your hormones into outer space – and there in outer space your hormones are being painted with all the magical genitals that a big penis porno star in heaven could ever imagine, and then the painting begins whispering all its exotic heresies to you, this is the painting that has been U*p*-cr**a**Wl*ing*-ar**O**u*nd* in your head for decades – this is the painting that's been *wanting wanting wanting* to CRASH out of your head and RAMPAGE upon the world! This is the painting filled with all the ecstasy of sin and war and peace and sex – it's a very special painting! It's a painting that marches with generations of ancestors... It's a painting where the colors have sex with each other and the colors are all having sex with the viewer – and the colors are all being created in a whorehouse –

It's a painting that THUMPS & THAWCKS & BAMS with the passion of a lover's jealousy... It's a painting as LOUD & MURDEROUS as the bullets *flying* from the war zones of the Middle East to the streetcorners of Chicago's Southside... It's a painting invading tomorrow with all the *n-i-g-h-t*-m-*a-r*-e-*s* that will BESIEGE the human race in the future... It's a painting whose seeds grow out of the corpses of the past...

You & I are now *surrounded* by this huge painting that's being created before our eyes... Except right now in front of you my body is *d-*

i-s-i-n-t-e-g-r-a-t-i-n-g into bodily fluids that are *flowing up* into the painting... All my bodily fluids are giving the painting life... The only thing that remains whole is my head that's being carried away by the arms of a living robot who's carrying hundreds of decapitated heads with him further & further into the painting. And I have no idea where my legs are – are they wandering around the painting?

And now, Vincent Van Gogh begins painting your face in millions of visions of misery that make you cry rivers of paint – and the rivers of Vincent Van Gogh's paint are flowing all over the planets surrounding us...

Then, Gaughin steals your penis and begins fucking all the women of the Polynesian islands with your penis, and out of all of his love-creations flow sensual colors & images & nudes & bellybuttons & vaginas & white & dark skin all creating a monstrous delight together!

And now your mouth has disappeared from your face! You look around you in amazement as your mouth reproduces itself thousands of times throughout the painting. Your mouth is saying these words right now. Your mouth is creating this painting.

And suddenly your eyes disappear from your head! Your eyes become thousands of eyes in the night sky staring down into the painting that's now SWALLOWING the world. Your eyes are helpless as your brains suddenly dissolve into the winds that are flying around inside the painting...

All the great painters of the past & present

both famous & unfamous are painting the

endless legions of a suffering wretched human

race... And you're crawling up all this suffering

human race into all of your thousands of eyes

in the sky that are all looking down upon you...

And as you're crawling up into the painting the

painting oozes diseases dribbling all over you...

You crawl up further & further into the

summits of the painting which seem both so

close and so far away...

And then suddenly you hear the voice of the

love of your life. And you see on top of the

corpses of your ancestors the naked body of

the love of your life and she's making love to

another man. And as your wife & her lover

FUCK & *moan* & *squeal* in JOY the painters

surround them and paint their lovemaking in all kinds of sensuous poses & colors. And you suddenly become so wrought with horrible feelings of *dread* & **a**-*n*-*x*-**i**-*e*-**T**-*y* & DEPRESSION & *sexual excitement* as you watch your wife's face in ecstasy... And you pull out your penis and begin *m*-**a**-*s*-**t**-*u*-**r**-**a**-*t*-**i**-*n*-**g** as you're watching this man making love to your wife. And the painters continue painting your wife & her lover and the painters smile at you now & then as they paint – it is a knowing smile – a mocking smile – a sympathetic smile – all CRASHING into one beautiful misery as suddenly colors & images *spurt* out of your penis and into the painting...

And one of the painters paints a symphony into existence and the orchestra plays to the rhythms of your wife & her lover making

ECSTASY together and the clarinet *laughs &*

laughs at you and the harp plays with the

sensuous rhythms & melodies of your wife's

lover pumping your wife full of his cock and the

violins join the rhyThms oF hiS In-&-oUt while

the cellos & double basses sTroKe baCk-&-

foRth with the rhYthms-of-yoUr-maSturbations

as you watch and then both the man & your

wife begin moaning & moaning and the

trumpet & the trombone begin *moaning &*

moaning with them and suddenly the

saxophone BLASTS out so *sensuously* as the

man cums & cums inside your wife...

And then your wife's lover walks away... He

disappears into the painting never to be seen

again. And then your wife sees you and smiles

at you with so much PLEASURE as you watch

the semen *flow* out of your wife's pussy and

the flute *joins* the melody as her lover's

overflowing semen *flows* out of your wife's

pussy and then you wife stands up and as the

piccolo & flute & birds *sing* together in the

most lovely colors your wife's tummy begins to

grow & grow and you walk over to your wife

and hug her from behind and you put your

arms around her with your hands resting on

her *growing* TUMMY and then there's a baby at

her breast as the oboe plays the sweetest

colors into existence...

And suddenly the entire symphony rises up in

a song of color, and the painters create all the

cheating couples of the world fornicating in a

swi*R*l*i*ng-m*a*sS*i*ve-t*O*r*n*ad*o*-hu*rr*ic*a*Ne that

rushes around & around the painting...

Phalluses & faces & buttocks & vaginas &

breasts all rushing around & around you as the

symphony plays & plays the painting into an

orgasm...

And then the painting becomes a giant face in

front of you – the painting becomes a giant

god staring at you with an open mouth as if it's

about to DEVOUR you, and then the god of the

painting DEVOURS the christian god, and all

the christians fall to their knees before the new

god in the painting whose face stairs upon

humanity without a sign of pity...

And the gigantic face in the painting becomes

as large as the planet Earth – and then the

face in the painting becomes as LARGE as the

sun – and the face in the painting becomes

larger & larger until the face in the painting is all anybody can see...

And the face of the painting speaks. The giant face in the painting does not speak in conventional language, but instead speaks in giant rivers of color flowing out of his mouth and the giant rivers of color are made out of words, the giant rivers are made out of orange words & yellow words & red words & blue words & green words & words of so many indescribable colors...

And the face of the painting opens its huge mouth and devours the reader, and suddenly the reader finds himself in the mind of the painting. The mind of the painting has the thoughts of every great painter that has ever lived. All the painters in the painter's mind are whispering millions of whispers of colors...

And now there are nudes – endless nudes – painted all over the walls surrounding you. The nudes painted on the walls talk to you, and you talk back to all the nudes painted on the wall.

Suddenly you find yourself in the midst of a giant white canvas all over again... You're all by yourself surrounded by this canvas that's suddenly empty again...

The sudden void of living inside a giant white canvas *terrorizes* you and you begin *running & running* for centuries trying to find something – ANYTHING! – but all you find is the endless white void of the painting all around you...

As the centuries pass you come to believe you will never see another human being again! You come to believe that this big white void surrounding you is all there is, you come to believe that the big white void is all there has ever been, you come to fear that it's all there will ever be! You wish there was something – *anything* in the world – besides this endless white canvas that COMPLETELY SURROUNDS you day after day after day...

And suddenly you hear someone *crying*. You are astounded! There is actually someone inside the painting with you!

You continue walking through the endless white void of the painting and you hear more cries. You're suddenly hearing so many voices crying in the white void of the empty canvas...

And you come across a man standing on a chair with a noose around his neck. He's *crying*. You SCREAM: "NO!"

But the man JUMPS anyway...

And suddenly the entire canvas goes black.

But now there are people all around you. But they are all black. Everyone is black. Even the white people are black. The sky above your head is black. Your own face & arms & hands are all black!

There is no sun anymore. The sun that used to infest the canvas with a great whiteness is now gone – the sun is gone forever! The blackness of the sky in the painting is again filled with billions & billions of your own eyes staring & staring at you for an eternity of misery...

And then all of a sudden everyone begins
SCREAMING black sounds and *whispering* black
sounds and s-p-e-a-k-*ing* in conversations of
black sounds. The orchestra begins playing.
But all the sounds that are created are black.
Endless black sounds everywhere...

And then a naked black woman walks into the
middle of the canvas. Giant bright colors JUMP
out of her! Everyone is suddenly bright colors
except for this beautiful naked black woman –
she *glows* with an immense vagina that *glows*
throughout the universe – a glorious vagina
that glows like the brightest star! She smiles at
you. You don't even know her. She says to you
with a smile: *"Let's make a baby!"*

She's wearing a mini-skirt, and her panties
come off like a wrapper off a candy bar. You

immediately start eating her pussy – it tastes so good! And she sucks your cock like a lollipop! 69! The whole painting loops & twists around in a huge 69 – the whole world & the painting rush & sing around each other in this psychedelic-color-69!

And as you're making a baby with this beautiful black woman the bright colors scream through the sky! The bright colors jump all over the canvas – and the artists smile as they paint the two of you making a baby together – bright happy colors jumping out of all the smiles of all the great artists that are painting the two of you making a baby together. And then you see your own wife watching the two of you and she's masturbating and colors are splashing out of her masturbations...

And the black woman below you whose legs are open to you and whose name you don't even know keeps saying: "*Let's make a baby! Let's make a baby!*" And as she says over & over again "*Let's make a baby let's make a baby!*" bright colors are flowing all over your naked bodies and bright colors such as have never existed before are percolating & boiling in your testicles and then you shoot millions & millions of paintings into her and suddenly her body explodes into bright colors flying everywhere...

You lay down exhausted, and you're feeling so good, and you watch as the colors of the sky repeatedly change color over & over again. The painters around you dip their brushes into the ever-changing colors of the sky, and they paint your portrait in every style of art that has ever

existed. They paint you as a child and they

paint you as an adolescent and they paint you

as an adult and they paint you on your

deathbed and then they paint you as a

corpse...

When you see them painting you as a corpse

you SCREAM and you _run away_ – but all the

corpses of you in the paintings JUMP OUT of

the paintings and _chase_ after you...

Suddenly your head opens! A smaller version

of yourself walks out of your head and begins

painting you. The painting of you walks out of

the canvas, and begins painting your wife &

your wife's lover. All the other painters begin

painting your wife & your wife's lover in so

many different colors & poses & art styles...

You immediately pull out your penis and begin *m-A-s-T-u-R-b-A-t-I-n-G*. The painters all begin singing colors to the rhythm of your *m-A-s-T-u-R-b-A-t-I-n-G*. Then the entire human race begins singing colors to the rhythm of you *m-A-s-T-u-R-b-A-t-I-n-G*. The painters are also painting to the rhythm of you *m-A-s-T-u-R-b-A-t-I-n-G*. The painters are all painting different portraits of you *m-A-s-T-u-R-b-A-t-I-n-G*.

The next day as you walk down the streets of your city there are paintings of you *m-A-s-T-u-R-b-A-t-I-n-G* hanging all over the walls of the city. In addition, everybody on the street walking by is carrying a painting of you *m-A-s-T-u-R-b-A-t-I-n-G*...

Suddenly all the laws of both society & government are replaced by art. Lawyers in court stop arguing about innocence & guilt and start creating paintings with their arguments. People stop driving according to traffic laws and start driving according to paintings.

People stop talking about the weather and other commonplace things and they start talking in bright colors, or sad colors, or they talk to each other in insane colors.

People no longer eat food. They begin eating images. People begin turning each other into images and cannibalizing each other...

Cannibalism is declared the highest form of art. And giant paintings celebrating cannibalism are hung up on all the plazas of all the cities of the world.

All cities no longer exist as physical entities. They become complex paintings. In these complex paintings you walk through millions & millions of smaller paintings within the larger painting. And then everything becomes a collage. All cities throughout the world become collages.

Then, in all the cities of the world everyone spontaneously throws off their clothes and poses naked on the streets for the painters. And the painters begin creating obscene collages of the orgies of mankind!

Yippee! Orgies!

No one sleeps anymore. No one exists anymore. Everyone is a different painting. Then each person multiplies into hundreds of paintings. Suddenly, all the paintings are making love to each other!

Then you pull all your wild emotions out of your guts & your brains & testicles. And you're spurting your wild emotions out of your penis! And all the painters are painting all your wild emotions in mathematical equations. The mathematical equations become philosophical inquiries that urinate imagery & colors all over the viewer...

And everyone begins vomiting their emotions all over the sky... And the painters begin painting all those emotions fornicating all over the canvas...

And everyone gathers over the corpse of the
christian god and begins urinating their
emotions all over his corpse as all the paintings
laugh & laugh and all the famous historical
figures of human history dig themselves out of
the ground and paint themselves into existence
and walk down the streets alongside of you –
you turn your head and there's Genghis Khan
& Julius Caesar both dressed up as
transvestites *laughing & skipping* down the
street together...

And even the streets cease to exist as reality:
the street loops up over the painting and into
another painting and out of that painting and
into another painting and the people are
walking in-and-out of all the paintings...

And as people talk to each other in the cafés the walls become insane landscapes that swallow the café, and the people in the painting on the walls talk to the people sitting in the café, and then the people in the café are SWALLOWED up into the paintings and become part of the paintings...

And the painting becomes the *greatest tidal wave of imagery* ever seen – the great tidal wave of this painting is *devouring* all of the Earth's continents – and everyone is DROWNING in a CHAOS of colorful imagery...

And the painting becomes pornographic – the painting becomes generations of desire & nudity & immaculate conception... And everyone JUMPS into the painting – everyone joins up with the orgy of imagery – an orgy

that EXPLODES with all the COLOR of six
billions – COLOR that's *created* by the great-
phallic-paintbrushes of the Artist-gods – even
the paintbrushes in the hands of women
become phalluses! And the great phalluses of
the artists begin creating a NEW WORLD – a
new APOCALYPSE– a great new pornographic
meaning for the human race who are all now
living inside the painting – this one painting is
a mountain of human flesh – this one painting
is the greatest ORGY to *excite* the human race!
–

And all around this painting – this great
painting that holds the human race in its arms
– this great orgy of color & art & flesh! –
around this painting is the swirling imagery
that's escaping from all of the artists' heads...

And the swirling imagery flying around the sky & the ground & your head is cumming from the orgasm of the painting – swirling-flying-imagery is flying out of your penis and into your head! – the painting becomes millions of penises all marching off into Christmas in a HAPPY-HAPPY-HAPPY of *ecstasy* – ecstasy being the sunny eclipse of art – art being the eternal flame of ecstasy...

Every human that has ever existed – that has ever loved – that has ever fought a war – that has ever helped build a house or a skyscraper with his own sweat – every human that has ever lived is in this painting!

In this painting all the *rhYthMs Of all thE wOrlD's mUsic* all JOIN TOGETHER in massive colorful orgasms – a living cast of bright colors

– everything is mOving-rhYthms-of-chaOs as the paintbrushes create millenniums of joy & war & procreation & poverty & disease all running around each other in the canvas...

The painting screeches with all the newborn babies of each generation growing old in a moment and making way for the next generation of screaming babies – it's all swimming there in the painting...

The painting is the wondrous saga of the great human race – the painting is this *vi*Olen*T*-*s*en*Su*al-st*ri*Vi*n*g-stor*Y* of man, this great story this great painting that ends with the approaching mushroom clouds, the painting pulses with 3.6 billion years of life until we become the dust of extinction... And that's when the painting cries out! That's when the painting dies! Because the painting dies when we die...

But for now, we are still breathing, we are still struggling, and the painting is the glory & strivings & suffering of a rickshaw puller in Calcutta India – his tremendous strength & power & energy is the strength & power & energy of this painting... Because this painting becomes larger with each new generation of humanity, because this painting is the story of each new generation, because this painting moves towards us in waves like the waves of the ocean splashing all over us – the painting splashes like gay sex all over us... The painting drowns us with its story... And the story of the painting is the story of generation after generation of the human race...

The painting speaks with 6 billion voices – the 6 billion voices that are our voices, the 6 billion voices of our species!

The painting is as dense & dark as the slums of Calcutta India. The painting is as fast as the assembly lines in Manaus Brazil, the painting throws its imagery – it's espresso-charged imagery jumps out of the traffic-clogged streets of the world – and now the viewer is being swallowed by this great cannibalistic painting...

The artists struggle to create this rampaging wave of imagery & color & rhythm that's flying out of the canvas – the artists are working as frenzied as those workers on the assembly line of the night shift –

Because the painting is 24 hours – because the painting never stops – because the painting is made out of every emotion that you have ever felt...

The painting breathes with you, the painting has its own rhythm – the painting has its own BEATS – just like the drums the painting has its own music – the painting beats to the same *rhythm* as your heart – the painting beats to the same *rhythm* as 6,000,000,000 hearts on this crowded planet...

The painting is filled with the NOISE of humanity: the construction sites, the machine guns speaking their own language of poetry in the inner cities & the front lines of war zones, the painting sings in color with a black Baptist choir, and the entire black Baptist congregation is being painted in sex & rhythm & American

negritude, the painting is filled with the colors

of *noise* of the BLAH BLAH BLAH in the cafés

and the dominoes PLOP-ing upon the tables

and the LOUD big buses SCREAMING down the

avenues and the YELLS & BRAWLS &

CLANGING of steel doors in prisons and the

huge monstrous toppick machines in the

world's ports ROAR-ing here & there and the

CLANKING-THUMPING sounds of moving

machinery in the factories – the painting

throws all these sounds about in LOUD

COLOR!...

In the painting sons & fathers are FIGHTING

each other, couples are SCREAMING at each

other, mother & daughter are SCOWLING at

each other, father & daughter are sharing

INCEST together – all the truths of "family

values" are parading out of the painting...

The painting is as high over your head as

1,000 grandiose imaginations stacked on top of

each other, the painting is as high as a

teenager smoking weed after school – out of

the painting roll the marijuana fields of

heaven, phrases of poetry with letters made

out of human limbs & bodies & heads...

The painting *splashes* with BLOOD as religions

FIGHT each other with swords & guns, the

lines of the painting *slash back-&-forth* with

the changing national boundaries of war, the

painting is as LOUD as war...

This is a painting that is FREE of the confines

of canvases & walls... This is a painting that is

not married to any past, this is a painting that arises out of the imaginations of all the creative greats, this is a painting that sings with many rhythms – that sings with many colors – that sings with many races of humanity all singing the painting together – a painting created by many voices – many paintbrushes – many songs – many histories – all weaving the entire human race together into the same painting...

The painting is so many tomorrows! The painting races up into the sky, which is where the future is! The painting does not confine itself to Earth, the painting is filled with the galaxies, the painting *is* the universe...

This painting is as big as the whole universe – and the painting is also as small as the smallest atom – the painting is a *sw-ir-ling*

dash of *at*Om*s* – the painting is the music of

atoms SWALLOWING each other and *dancing*

around each other and *fornicating* with each

other – this is what the painting is!

The heroin addicts fly through the painting like

astronauts & cosmonauts making homoerotic

outerspace jazz together, the sailors sail their

boats through the painting, the fisherman

catch words from the painting, the farmers

harvest words from the painting – the words

are to be eaten by the human race as poetry

because painting & poetry are incestuous twins

having sex all over the canvas, the painting *r-*

r-r-r-r-rr-rr-rrrr-rr-s like the moving machinery

that the painting is, because the painting is a

giant machine, because the painting is a giant-

BEATING-heart,,,

And humanity races *back-and-forth* from one

end of the painting to the other, humanity

grabs buses and drive cars from one end of the

painting to the other, because the painting is a

dripping blood field of human lives all

CLASHING & *loving* & KILLING together...

The painting is *r*i*v*eR*s*-of-*b*aBbl*ing-n*eO*n-*

*s*Yll*ab*Le*s* because the paint *dribbles* and *flows*

with the alcohol that *dribbles* and *flows*

through the bars, the painting is a caricature of

all the *fac*E**s** in all the bars of the world, the

painting is a c*a*R*i*CaT**u***re* of all the fAc*e*S on all

the Manhattan streets & avenues *flowing in*

and out of the painting... The painting is a

c_a_RiCaTu_re_ of all the faces walking down all
the streets of the world...

You HATE the painting like an enemy that you
must KILL, you _love_ the painting like a woman
that you want to make babies with, you _kiss_
the painting like you _kiss_ a woman's breasts,
you hold the painting in your arms the same
way you hold a woman in your arms with so
much LUST & LOVE because LOVE & LUST is
what you _feel_ for the painting, the LOVE &
LUST that _rises up_ within the artists and makes
them PASSIONATE as they _throw_ all their
passion into the creation of the painting...

The painting is bigger than any one artist, the
painting flows together with all the creative
energies of a thousand great artists, there is
no beginning & no end of the painting, the

imagery of one artist mingles & fornicates with

the imagery of the other artists, and it all

bubbles forth out of the canvas like the

sweetest decadence & violence that has ever

touched your lips...

Slashing right through the middle of the

painting is a war zone, the war zone between

the two races of white & black *slashing* through

the South Side of Chicago, the painting *rising*

up out of the canvas with BLOOD – the same

BLOOD that has fallen on every street corner

on Chicago's South Side, and the painting is

also a mixture of different races of semen

racing across the giant canvas – the same

spermatozoa that has mixed all the races &

ethnic groups on Chicago's South Side – the

painting is made out of all this blood &

semen...

The painting was conceived in a hot bedroom

overlooking an alleyway on Chicago's South

Side over four decades ago, the painting was

conceived when the first two amoebas

conceived in the ocean some 4,000,000,000

years ago to later become fish & amphibians &

then rats & monkeys and then you & me – we

are all the painting – the reader & the writer

are both in the painting together...

The painting blasts off the Earth and into outer

space for the first time on October 4, 1957

with Sputnik, in the middle of the painting is

Yuri Gagarin's smile as he becomes the first

human to look upon the earth from outer

space, because every great human

achievement is a part of the painting, the
October Revolution of 1917 holds the most
special place within the painting, the portraits
of Marx & Engels & Lenin & Trotsky hold the
most honored places within the painting, from
the upper reaches of the painting Marx &
Engels & Lenin & Trotsky look upon a
struggling working class fighting for a better
future...

And all of the different elements of the painting
are all *fighting* each other, the colors are all
fighting each other, the rhythms are all
fighting each other, the people in the painting
are all *fighting* each other, the imagery in the
painting CRASHES & COLLIDES into each other
with TREMENDOUS NOISE – because this is a
new kind of painting...

This is not a painting you can buy, this is not a painting that you can stick up in an art gallery and put a price on, a bourgeoisie cannot horde this painting in his living room where nobody else can see it, because this painting is everywhere and belongs to everyone...

And the painting *sings* with the INTERNATIONAL...

The painting looks at you with its endless eyes – the painting looks at you with the eyes of the human race – the painting holds you in its billions of arms and the painting throws you into millions of directions and the painting throws you off into other solar systems and the painting shows you other people's lives – the painting shows you the personal intricacies of 6 billion lives all weaving into a gigantic whole...

And as you're drowning in the painting you reach up your arms to the sky – to the night sky – and the night sky pulls you up into an opposite painting – in the opposite painting gravity drips up into the sky like hallucinogenic coffee, and everything in the painting flows out of the universe... In the opposite painting outerspace is swimming in spermatozoa, and the planets are all inverse vaginas that swallow entire solar systems and turn them into the colors that constantly feed the ever-hungry painting...

The painting pulls you everywhere into as many emotions & expressionist modes of painting as there are people on the planet – the painting launches you into all kinds of impossibilities that exist beyond words – the painting lands you in all kinds of different solar systems where life thrives in an endless variety of *bi*Z*arre-co*L*orful-f*O*rms*...

Because the painting is everything that you have seen, and the painting is everything out there that you have not yet seen...

The painting *shoots* through you with all the *energy* of a double espresso! The painting *thrives* with all the ENERGY of a personal strip-tease by a sexy beautiful woman (or sexy handsome man) in your own bedroom...

And the painting CLASHES & *thrashes* with *blood* & SWORDS & *spears* as new world & old world meet together in a CLASHING of civilizations...

And now the painters of the world begin

painting everybody completely naked – all six

billions of humanity in the flesh – the painters

paint vaginas as wide as the universe and

nipples as pink as your mother's vagina, the

painters paint all our hormones lavishing

through our bodies – the painters paint the

horny dog of the inner souls of both men &

women throughout the world...

The painters paint all the youthful thrilling joy

of young couples *kissing* & *kissing* in all of the

parks & plazas of Latin America – their lips

glued to each other in hours & hours of lustful

adolescent naughtiness, the paintbrushes

capture all this as the paintbrushes move like

giant storms across the canvases – the

paintbrushes move like fingers across naked

bodies as the painters paint everyone's naked

bodies with waterfalls of desire...

Together, the painters create a constant

pornography...

And the painters are painting orgies in the

whorehouses/city halls of America where the

wealthy citizenry & the politicians share

intimacy & money & influence, the painters

paint politicians bending over on their desks

with their pants down as the corporate leaders

of America have their way with the elected

leaders in the whorehouses/city halls/state

legislatures across the country...

The painters paint all the WORRY all over the

face of a pregnant adolescent named Maria –

and whether that Maria lived 2,000 years ago

in the Middle East or today in Latin America the painters paint all of her SUFFERING & *angst* of a pregnant Maria carrying an unwanted child whose name will be Jesus, and the painters paint the hunger of the baby in her tummy because she doesn't have enough money to eat...

The painters paint shantytowns surrounding the big cities of the Third World, the painters paint the endless dark misery of the human condition for half the world's population, century after century of SUFFERING...

The painters paint yearning & destruction & love & procreation...

The painters paint a giant man in a hard hat who is black on one side of his face and white

on one the other side of his face – and his
giant arms reach up to the sky – the broken
chains of his liberation falling from his half-
white half-black body – and below him the
painters paint the rising human race – the
rising working-class – the painters paint
revolutions percolating throughout the world...

The painters paint the French nobility being led
to the guillotines as the masses cheer for
more! The painters paint the French commune
and the October Revolution of 1917 – and the
painters paint general strikes throughout the
world...

The painters paint heavy industry and
automobiles and highways and train tracks and
every other form of great human progress...

The painters paint *hunger* – the painters paint HUNGER *infesting* the human race – the painters paint hunger as endless monsters screaming in people's bellies...

The painters paint all the churning wheels of drug addiction t*urn*i*n*g-t*urn*i*n*g-t*urn*i*n*g in the drug addict's mind – the painters paint all the endlessness of WANT – all the hammer-hammer-hammering of a ticking-ticking-ticking NEED that infests your thoughts minute after minute hour after hour until you give in to your addiction calling – your addiction calling you over & over again like some incessant telephone *ringing & ringing* 24 hours a day with a*ddi*Ctio*n*-a*ddic*Tion-a*d*Dicti*On!*

The painters paint endless bars, the bars where the hookers throw their vaginas & tits at potential customers, the bars where blue-collar

hardhats drink their misery & happiness & hard

lives in an alcohol ocean of comraderie, the

bars where the rich ugly old men meet the

pretty young ladies, the bars where the college

students drink & laugh & drink some more

amongst all the loud music & louder

hormones...

The painters paint the human race under a

clock with five minutes to midnight, the

painters paint the future nuclear mushroom

clouds swallowing the world, the painters paint

billions of screaming faces inside the

mushroom clouds, the painters paint all the

cities of the world being engulfed being

swallowed being eaten by the monstrous

mushroom clouds...

The painters paint the couples in a super

relaxed state after their orgasms, the painters

paint the wonderful void of the human body &

mind after the orgasm, the painters paint

orgasms all over the human race, the painters

paint orgasms all over the cities...

The painters paint so many people

masturbating behind closed doors & walls, the

painters paint hands & penises and the

rhythmic magic of dildos & vaginas in rooms

across the world, and the painters paint the

fetishes, like the men watching their wives

being fucked by their lovers, the artists paint

all the exotic whipping & spanking in the S &

M-bedroom-dudgeons across the world...

The painters paint naked bodies & whips &

high heels & dominatrixes, the painters paint

men fucking each other up the ass and sucking

each other's cocks, the painters paint women

eating each others' vaginas in glorious 69's...

The painters paint a tidal wave of sex over the

human race – a tidal wave of sex over the

cities – a tidal wave of sex over the world...

Penises & war and pussy & death is the

constant rhythm of the painting... The painters

paint Uncle Sam vomiting wars across the

world, the painters paint the laughing US

president in an airplane defecating bombs

across Afghanistan & Vietnam – the bombs

falling out of the President's anus onto the

screaming people below...

The artists paint preachers snorting cocaine

before they give their sermons, the artists

paint priests having sex with altar boys & other men's wives, the painters paint the Pope with the devil's face, the painters paint born-again Christians with horns & hooves & tails & pitchforks, the artists paint all the born-again Christians in hell...

The artists paint 6 million Jews going up through the smokestacks, the painters paint the German capitalists giving Adolf Hitler mountains of money, the painters paint Latin American death squads shooting down peasants & workers with American bullets...

The painters paint the housing projects of America – these 20-30-40 story hells rising up through the sky, and in these housing projects the artists paint so many black suffering faces... The painters paint four centuries of

suffering black faces throughout American
history...

The painters paint soldiers slashing each other
to death with bayonets and blood feeding the
ever-hungry land, the painters paint god's
spermatozoa swimming down from the sky and
into the vagina of the Virgin Mary, then the
painters paint the Virgin Mary opening her legs
to a Roman soldier & then the baker & then the
street merchant – the painters paint the Virgin
Mary's face in ecstasy as she receives the seed
of God from whoever gave it to her...

The painters paint God as a muscular
transvestite with a humongous beard *dancing*
in heaven to 24-hour LOUD LOUD polka music,
the painters paint Jesus Christ suffering &
dying on the cross as the Pope & the priest &

the preachers gather around him below and

laugh & laugh & laugh... The painters paint the

Pope wearing luxurious gold as he stands

below a suffering dying Jesus Christ, the

painters paint greasy television preachers

fucking each other up the butt and sucking

each other's cocks amidst a sea of money...

And the murals begin jumping off the walls and

becoming reality! And the people in all the

paintings become real and all the real people

walking down the street become part of the

paintings and the paintings jump into each

other and become a *mi*X-m**a**T*ch*-

c*orn*Oc**a**peLi*a*-**o**f-*cra*Zi*ne*S*s* and this *mi*X-

m**a**T*ch*-c*orn*Oc**a**peLi*a*-**o**f-*cra*Zi*ne*S*s* becomes a

new hyper-normality exploding with

LAUGHTER...

Because normality is being painted out of existence! Because all the BRIGHT COLORS of our *emotions* are what the sky is born for every day! The painters paint everything on the earth that's UGLY until the most UGLY UGLINESS is piled on top of each other! Even everything beautiful is painted ugly *ugly* UGLY– because UGLY is *beautiful* and *beautiful* is UGLY!

Because your face in the painting my love is as beautiful and as ugly as Santa Claus & a gorilla at the zoo taking turns fucking each other up the butt! And the painters create years and years of ugliness! And everyone on the planet gets on their knees before this beautiful ugliness that is the painting and exclaims "IT'S TIME FOR US TO SHIT THE PAINTING ALL

OVER THE CANVAS! WE DEMAND MASS ART

DIARRHEA!"

The painters paint all the OH NO GODDAMMIT

of old age, they paint all the random MADNESS

of *sickness* & *disease* – endless corpses

stacked around the painting – nothing ugly in

the world escapes the eyes of the painters!

In the painting the bourgeoisie are painted as

pigs – as are all the politicians too, and the

police are painted as German shepherds &

Doberman pinchers & Rottweilers in blue

uniforms...

The painting THROBS & *pulses* with all the

young ladies showing off their new tits with

tight shirts – all their childhood innocence &

vulnerability & a*d*Ol*e*S*c*e**n**t-ho**R***m***o**nal-*d*eSire*s*

GROWING like sexual fruit throughout the painting – because life is BURSTING with everything! Because youth is BURSTING with everything! Because youth is BURSTING with ripeness & wild savagery & endless mountains of sex!

Because every new dawn BURSTS with a million *hopes* in every city, and every new Saturday night is BURSTING with sex & fun & drunkenness & wild rhythms – and the painting EXPLODES with all of this! The painting EXPLODES with all the *energy* of every new dawn and all the *energy* of every new Saturday night!

The painting is always *jumping* out from behind the reader, the painting is always *traveling* thousands of miles an hour head on

at the reader! The painting *runs around &
around* the reader for 24 hours a day every
day of the year – the reader sleeps with the
painting's arms around the reader and the
painting is the reader's dreams & nightmares,
and while the reader is awake the daylight
shines from the painting like a tingling
sexually-transmitted disease...

The colors JUMP OFF the clothes of the
passerby – and the colors JUMP OFF all the
advertisements & graffiti – the colors JUMP
OFF of everything around us – and the colors
become all the sexual abstractions with a life
of their own!

You SCREAM the painting! And now everyone
is SCREAMING the painting! And now everyone
is *whispering* the painting at each other –

everyone *whispers* a different phrase of the painting, and all these different phrases of the painting join together as one, and now the painting walks all around you...

The painting SCREAMS at you! The painting SCREAMS at everyone!

And the piano keys roll up & down the painting as the painting *travels* around the music as the harp *creates* sensual colors and the trumpet BLURTS out a color revolution and the saxophone plays with the colors like a *masturbatory itch* constantly *begging* for color between our legs and the drums are BASHING the colors out at you like *swinging* baseball bats SMASHING all the colorful world into existence!

Floods of humanity CRASH & *laugh* & *sing* out of the painting! So many faces protruding out of this painting... Streets & crowds & music all *pouring out* of the painting... Everything all CLASHING out of the painting as all the trumpets & saxophones & trombones play the painting into millions of colorful emotions...

And everyone falls to their knees before the painting because the painting is a religion... Because all the excellent sins ravaging through our genitals are part of the painting – all the eternal sins of neo-classicism playing with all the COLOR COLOR COLOR – and the painting is the new religion of sin – because art is a new religion – because sin is the new religion – because art is the greatest religion – because together Darwin and art decapitate God!

This and all the colors of this painting are
falling out of God's decapitated head as the
Devil *sodomizes & sodomizes* the decapitated
corpse of God – and as the Devil sodomizes
the corpse of God the devil *laughs & laughs* in
colors cascading out of his LAUGHTER like
neon waterfalls of sin & bliss...

And suddenly the entire Earth *shakes* with
EARTHQUAKES and giant bright color *thrashes*
everywhere out of the ground and drowns the
landscape in painting, and suddenly part of the
painting EXPLODES and *drowns* the universe in
the blood of the painting...

And painting becomes a form of dying and
rebirth... As one generation of painters falls &
dies the next generation of painters grabs the
paintbrushes of the newly fallen and begins

painting the never-ending masterpiece of the

painting – this is the painting that the entire

human race is creating together – a

masterpiece painted by a thousand

generations! A masterpiece as large as 6 billion

minds being thrown on canvas...

Because insanity is painting, because suddenly

everyone on the planet is taken up with

insanity and everyone on the planet grabs a

paintbrush and begins throwing all their

insanities all over the walls & sidewalks & each

other in insane dripping hormones of *color-*

color-color! Because we must worship insanity!

Because insanity is art and art is insanity!

And one of the painters vomits up all his

insanity... And now all the buildings of the city

are d-r-i-p-p-i-n-g with his insanity & vomit &

art.... Because insanity & vomit & art are all becoming a ménage à trois performing Fernard Leger orgies all over the canvas, because the canvas is the world, because the world is a giant canvas that we are creating with our paintbrushes!

And now we throw the *sweetness* of a smiling young virgin all over the canvas, and we throw the an*geR* & *mEnaCi*ng-m*uR*d*er*O*us*-th*ough*T**s** of a soldier about to go into battle all over the canvas as well, in the canvas we throw all the FEAR of a newly evicted family standing in the street with all their possessions – because the canvas is ANGER & *feeeeaaaaar* – because the canvas is a WAR of different i*ma*G*e*s & c*o*L*o*r**s** & **a**R*t* m**O**vem**E**n*ts* all *slashing & slashing* into each other in a VIOLENT HALLUCINATION all

over the canvas...

The painting wants to cuddle with the reader,

the painting wants to make love to the reader,

the painting wants to penetrate the reader with

all of its *su*iCi*des* & *h*Omi*c*idEs & fR**a**triCi*des*!

As the reader surrenders him/herself to the

painting she feels the ecstasy of colors

traveling throughout her body, she feels the

painting growing in her tummy, she feels the

painting as a *wet-warm-squishyness* inside her

pussy, she surrenders herself completely to the

painting over & over again...

And all of the women's pussies and all of the

man's anuses are all ravaged by the giant

paintbrushes of the great painters, the great

painters are now worshiped as sex gods! And

all the women want to procreate with the painters and carry their love child for nine months...

And the next generation of the human race are the offspring of only artists, because that's exactly the way it should be!

So the Artists conquer the world! And so the Artists are declared kings & gods! And so all men surrender their wives to the great Artists, and all of this luscious Eden of procreation helps the Artists to create ever more orgies of art & sex on ever more planets, because art is a form of FORNICATION, because FORNICATION is a form of art...

And now the artists form separate armies, and the artists begin attacking the canvas with their paintbrushes, and the canvas becomes

multiple armies of artists and art styles all

fighting each other across the canvas...

The landscape throws itself through the giant

canvas and creates hundreds of giant canvases

one behind the other. Suddenly, we are not

sure where the canvas begins and the world

ends, and where the world begins and where

the canvas ends...

In the painting the ground grows THOUSANDS

of *snakes* of _e_MoTioN*s* – the paintbrushes paint

space stations, and the paintbrushes paint

whole planets inhabited by the gi*a*N**t**-pe*n*iS-

ciTi*es* of h*u*Ma*ns* – the painting CELEBRATES

human beings as the great PRIMATES – the

greatest of all PRIMATES... The most intelligent

of PRIMATES ever!

Lust grows out of the painting like the most degenerate kind of sinuous luxury, penises & vaginas are everywhere in the painting! In the painting women's orgasms are portrayed as erotic messages from God, in the painting millions of giant male phalluses are growing out of the corpse of God, in the painting the Virgin Mary is a fertility goddess whose sexual lust for semen satisfies the lust of sailors throughout the world, in the painting Jesus Christ is painted in a homosexual bathhouse giving everyone blow jobs – muscular men circling around Jesus to get their fair share of blow jobs from the son of God!

EVERYONE in the painting has giant vaginas growing out of them – even the men! Everyone in the painting has giant phalluses growing out of them – even the women!

In the painting the bourgeoisie wait in line behind the French aristocracy at the guillotines, in the painting there are giant Aztec & Mayan temples where the bourgeoisie & their prostitute-politicians are being sacrificed for the glory of the Artist & Proletarian gods!

The entire painting is painted in the rhythms of WAR & STRIKES & REVOLUTIONS & CIVIL WARS all *thundering & thundering* with the painting, and then the painting becomes *silence* and all the painters paint the great SILENCE, and then the painting *dances* with a thousand different songs from all over the world...

The painting simultaneously leads the readers
& viewers through thousands of different
hallways where all the walls are the graffiti-
creations of *in*S**a***n*e-aR*t*ist-hoO*d*lum-**a***r*T-
jU*n*kie*s*, the painting throws the reader's mind
through these thousands of different hallways
where the *in*S**a***n*e-aR*t*ist-hoO*d*lum-**a***r*T-jU*n*kie*s*
have ANONYMOUS SEX with each other in
couples & groups and they live to have SEX
and *create art*, they talk in colors, they
SCREAM in art movements, they *sex* in
COLORS, they NIGHTMARE in canvases, they
dream in erotic phrases of poetry intertwined
with phalluses & anuses & pussies like a
growing vine of Celtic art...

And the *in*S**a***n*e-aR*t*ist-hoO*d*lum-**a***r*T-jU*n*kie*s*
EAT the walls off the buildings and SHIT the

walls into the painting and the walls are used

as giant canvases of the me*n*tallY-ILL-m*i*lliO**n**s,

and the hordes of me*n*tallY-ILL-m*i*lliO**n**s are

joined by the *in*Sa*n*e-aR*t*ist-hoO*d*lum-a*r*T-

jU**n**kie*s* who all begin ATTACKING passerby

with art, they begin ATTACKING society with

art, they ASSAULT politicians with art, they

KILL the bourgeoisie with art, they announced

the dictatorship of the Artists & Workers...

And the Artists & the Workers together create

the great new dawn of art & humanity,

together they create the greatest WONDER

ever known to mankind... They create the

endless painting that is always *growing* &

growing...

And the newborn babies SCREAM with art, and on their deathbeds the dying *whisper* art into the ears of their gathered-around loved ones...

And the canvas suddenly begins spontaneously *growing* nipples & bellybuttons – even though the artists didn't put them there – and now the artists are confused...

And the workers on the night shift of the painting paint the painting with blues & slow rhythms & the endless century of the night that *drifts* into the painting like *flowing* midnights... And the workers on the day shift paint the painting as a *fast-fast-schizophrenic-roaring-assembly-line of daydreams*, because the painting is both these things – the painting is ALL things...

The painting shows napalm raining down on Vietnam – the painting shows the SCREAMING Vietnamese people with napalm *burning* through their skin – the painting shows the American soldiers with their bayonets *slicing* through the ribs of Vietnamese men & women & children – the painting shows millions of Japanese in a rising mushroom cloud over Hiroshima & Nagasaki, the painting shows the predator drones over Afghanistan & Pakistan & Yemen, the painting shows the American bombs raining down all over Vietnam & Afghanistan & Pakistan, the painting shows the American Empire built on a world full of blood & corpses & skulls...

The painting shows the American Empire starving the nations of Iraq & Cuba with economic embargoes, the painting shows the American Empire with its bombs falling all over the world, with its troops invading nations across the planet, with the black chattel-slaves working the fields and the white wage-slaves (including children!) working the textile mills & other factories, and above all this human misery sit the capitalist pigs in their luxurious penthouse heavens where they sit amongst piles of money...

Suddenly half the painting is the black ghettos of inner-city America with their abandoned buildings & empty lots & empty storefronts – the painting seethes with the desperation of inner-city ghetto America – and the other half of the painting are industrial towns with abandoned factory buildings and the empty storefronts of Main Street America where white

passerby walk by with sad & desperate faces...

The painting shows much of the American

Midwest rusting & abandoned – rusting heavy

industry everywhere – abandoned buildings

everywhere, unemployed white & black faces

everywhere...

The painting shows the abandoned family

farms across the country, and big corporate

agriculture feeding ground-up dead cows to

living cows (cannibalistic cows!), the painting

shows the endless growth hormones & other

chemicals being dumped into the feed of pigs &

chickens, the painting shows the fattening of

pigs & chickens & the American people...

And half the painting shows a white family being evicted from their home and the other half of the painting shows a black family being evicted from their home and the painting shows the MISERY of the children being evicted from their homes and the painting shows their *river of tears* joining up with the *river of tears* of the Afghanistani & Vietnamese & Iraqi people *flowing* through the canvas and out into the world in a river of misery...

And half the painting shows the life of a white industrial worker and the other half of the painting shows the life of a black industrial worker and the painting shows their woes – their GIGANTIC WORRIES – the unaffordable medical bills – the mortgage chained around their necks – the high taxes on their backs –

and the painting shows their tax money going into the coffers of big corporations in endless bailouts...

And the painting shows the black nationalists & white supremacists as rodents – the black nationalist whispering lies & filth into the ear of the black worker as he points with hostility at the white worker – and the white supremacist whispering lies & filth into the ear of the white worker as he points with hostility at the black worker...

And the rich & powerful *laugh & laugh* as white & black & Latino workers are divided against each other – DIVIDE & CONQUER!

The white supremacists & black nationalists are portrayed as groups of rodents attacking interracial couples & Jews & immigrants, and in the painting is a Korean grocery store and in front of the Korean grocery store on the right side is a group of white supremacists painted as rodents picketing the Korean grocery store while on the left side of the painting is a group of black nationalists painted as rodents also picketing the Korean grocery store...

And then the painting shows Hitler and the SS as rats receiving huge amounts of money from German capitalists painted as pigs, Hitler & the Gestapo & the German capitalists are doing their business together on a mountain of human skulls & bones while the German capitalist pigs feast on human beings & profits...

The painting shows Democratic politicians painted as donkeys wearing the white robes of the Ku Klux Klan, and the painting shows police officers wearing white hoods, and the painting shows a black man hanging from the tree while Democratic politicians like George "segregation forever" Wallace & Barack Obama & Delano Roosevelt & John F. Kennedy all smile under the black man hanging from the tree amongst the crowd of Ku Klux Klaners...

And the painting shows prison walls being built around America and all of the Americans are wearing orange prison suits, the entire nation is painted as a huge penitentiary...

And every nation on earth is then painted as a huge penitentiary, (although each one with its own individual characteristics), every nation on earth is painted with a group of pigs at the top

(capitalists, politicians, dictators), and beneath

the pigs are painted judges whose faces are a

giant pair of buttocks, and below the judges

are painted attack dogs wearing police

uniforms, and the attack dogs in police

uniforms are beating & shooting all the

working people & poor, and the working people

& poor are at the bottom and it is upon their

shoulders & backs that rest the tower of Babel

that includes the police & judges & capitalist

pigs & politicians & dictators...

And the painting shows a series of panels

where two Black Panthers by the names of

Mark Clark & Fred Hampton are sleeping while

a horde of police goons surround their building

and suddenly the painting shows the bullets

flying and the blood gushing as the police –

who are painted as German Shepherds &

Rottweilers & Doberman pinchers in blue

uniforms – smile around the corpses of Mark

Clark & Fred Hampton...

And the painting paints Mark Clark & Fred

Hampton & all the other Black Panthers as

heroes in the struggle for black liberation...

And the painting becomes all the tidal waves of

violence of the American Civil War – Civil War

bullets flying out of the painting everywhere!

The painting becomes a northern Civil War

soldier charging into the Confederate lines –

bullets flying past him and his buddies falling

all around him – and then his bayonet is

slashing through a Confederate soldier as

blood & cannon explosions fly all around him...

And then the painting shows that northern Civil War soldier – so FRUSTRATED so ANGRY so DESPERATE– pointing his rifle at a fleeing slaveowner and – BLAM! – The northern soldier smiles as the slaveowner falls to the ground...

The painting shows that moment where the northern soldier & his comrades march onto a plantation and announce to all the curious black faces: "YOU'RE FREE!"

And the painting shows the northern soldier at that moment where his eyes fall upon a beautiful black woman and her lovely eyes fall upon him too as she smiles so sweetly and then the painting shows them making love somewhere in the fields when suddenly the black woman's boyfriend shows up and the northern Civil War soldier and the black man fight with fists...

The painting celebrates the great heroic Sherman's March through the South! The painting rises up with the faces of the hundreds of thousands of northern white men who gave their lives so that black people could be free! So that the Confederacy – so that the slavocracy – could be smashed into pieces and burned to the ground...

The painting celebrates the burning of Atlanta as the most beautiful necessity! Rising above the painting is a gigantic portrait of William Tecumseh Sherman – William Tecumseh Sherman the great American hero! William Tecumseh Sherman is painted as the god of the Civil War that he is!

And underneath this greatness of the bust of William Tecumseh Sherman are painted all of the brave men both white & black who wore the blue Civil War uniform of the North during the Civil War – because they are even MORE heroic than William Tecumseh himself!

And the painting shows the great deeds of Reconstruction! The painting shows the black people freeing themselves of their chains and voting and opening businesses and running for political office – the painting shows the heroic black people rising to the occasion of Reconstruction...

And then the painting shows the Democrats – represented as a bunch of good-old-boy laughing asses (or donkeys) – the painting shows the Democrats viciously attacking

Reconstruction – the painting shows the Democrats and the Ku Klux Klan and the local police as a united one lynching and attacking the black people...

And the painting shows the neo-slavery of sharecropping where the black people work the cotton fields and the white people work in the textile mills – white children working at machines in northern textile mills – while the capitalist pigs eat caviar & drink champagne amidst mountains of money...

And the painting shows the waves of immigrants arriving in America being crowded into inner-city slums – dark wretched slums teeming with humanity – and the painting shows the Protestant Anglo-Saxon bigots attacking Catholic immigrants...

And the painting shows the heroic struggles of the Irish people – starved in Ireland by the Anglo-Saxon landowners who stole the land from the Irish, and then proceeded to export food grown on the stolen land while the Irish people starved – the painting shows the same ships that were used to transport African slaves later being used to transport the Irish immigrants – so many Irish immigrants dying in the great ocean passage – the painting shows the bones of the African & Irish people mixing at the bottom of the Atlantic ocean...

And the painting begins to show that the Irish story is only one of many stories that burns throughout immigrant America – that same story that burns through many ethnic Americans who have heard of the nightmare that their immigrant ancestors had to bear –

and the painting shows Latino immigrants

bearing that same nightmare today...

The painting shows Wolf Larsen as a kid on the

Southside of Chicago beating up bullies & black

nationalists & white supremacists, the painting

shows the white blonde-haired blue-eyed Wolf

Larsen and his black high school sweetheart

*kiss*ing & *kiss*ing & *kiss*ing everywhere –

*kiss*ing in the high school hallways *kiss*ing in

the parks *kiss*ing on the lakefront *kiss*ing

downtown *kiss*ing in his home and the painting

shows Wolf Larsen beating up *more* black

nationalists & white supremacists...

The painting shows Wolf Larsen as a kid

smashing through anything that got in his way

when he was running for the touchdown,

because Wolf Larsen was a clueless skill-less brute who didn't bother running around his opponents on the football field – Wolf Larsen SMASHED through ANYTHING that got in his way!

And the painting itself SMASHES through everything that gets in its way...

Wolf Larsen didn't care about race – WHA!M WHA!M BA!M – Wolf Larsen kicked the ass of both black nationalists & white supremacists with equal happiness... And if there was a whole bunch of black nationalists or white supremacists wanting to kick Wolf Larsen's ass – well then, Wolf Larsen could ruuuuuuuun – you ain't seen nothin' faster than Wolf Larsen running from a group of black nationalists or white supremacists on the South Side of

Chicago...

The painting shows all the hatred on the South

Side of Chicago fading and being replaced by

the brightest of colors as Wolf Larsen kisses his

beautiful black high school sweetheart, the

painting shows Wolf Larsen's daydreams of his

beautiful black high school sweetheart in a

white wedding dress, and then a dozen of the

most beautiful interracial children...

The painting shows Wolf Larsen holding so

many women in his arms – holding so many

women from so many different races &

countries in his arms – but all the women have

the beautiful black face of his high school

sweetheart, even the white women in Wolf

Larsen's arms have the beautiful black face of his high school sweetheart...

The waves of Lake Michigan all have endless beautiful faces of his high school sweetheart, the sun in the sky has the face of Wolf's high school sweetheart, the moon has the face of his high school sweetheart, the painting becomes 1,000 variations of the white Wolf Larsen and his black high school sweetheart making love...

Suddenly the painting is filled with white men and black women making love... Their naked bodies moving deliciously in-&-out of each other in a fascinating contrast of color & light...

And then the painting is filled with black men & white women making love for century after century of bliss, white women's faces filled

with joy as black men fuck them for hours &

hours of happiness...

And the painting is filled with both white men &

black women and black men & white women

getting married, and having babies, and having

grandchildren, and hugging each other, and

growing old together...

And suddenly the painting shows restaurants

filled with interracial couples, where the streets

are filled with interracial couples, because

there is nothing more beautiful than interracial

love, because there is no baby more beautiful

than an interracial baby...

And suddenly the painting becomes gigantic

with a black man and a white woman holding

up a beautiful interracial baby, and all the
bright colors of the world emanate from their
beautiful interracial baby...

And suddenly the white Wolf Larsen & his
beautiful black high school sweetheart are at
the top of an Aztec-Mayan temple holding up
their beautiful interracial baby under the
dawning sun, and the entire human race gets
on their knees before the greatness of their
beautiful interracial baby...

And the painting is suddenly filled with the
white Wolf Larsen & his beautiful black high
school sweetheart making a baby together,
and endless bright colors and happy colors and
blissful colors all splash out of their
lovemaking...

And the painting becomes a happiness of Art Nouveau as a white Wolf Larsen and his beautiful black high school sweetheart walk through the park together hand-in-hand with her tummy so big...

And suddenly all the lovemaking of the white Wolf Larsen and his beautiful black high school sweetheart becomes a new religion of immaculate conception, and Wolf Larsen's high school sweetheart becomes the world's most beautiful fertility goddess, and churches – beautiful sinful churches filled with erotic imagery – are built throughout the world – and in these churches everyone can practice the rites of immaculate conception under the smiling gaze of the white Wolf Larsen and his black high school sweetheart...

And the walls of all the churches shall be painted with the white Wolf Larsen and his black high school sweetheart making love, and the walls of these churches shall also be painted with black men making love to white women, and also with men making love to men, and with women making love to women, the walls of these churches shall be painted with the entire human race making love to each other...

And under the smiling gaze of the white Wolf Larsen and his beautiful black high school sweetheart the orgies of the human race shall begin, and instead of being used for armaments money will be used for AIDS research, and once the cure is found everyone will be creating beautiful immaculate conceptions with complete strangers in the temples of the white Wolf Larsen and his beautiful black high school sweetheart...

And everything will be painted with sensuous colors and naked bodies making love – even the subway trains will be painted with naked bodies – *everything* will be painted with sex – and glorious sensuous sculptures of people making love will adorn all the public buildings & parks – and in the parks everyone will be making love – and in the offices everyone will be making love during lunch hour & coffee breaks – and nobody will care whose kid is whose – because all kids will be raised communally...

So the painting runs around with a 24-hour rhythm of night and day – the painting weaves together a 24-hour rhythm of neon and dawn

and work and play and sleep and sex and

youth and old-age and desperation and hope...

The painting grows distressed with all the

money worries of all the millions, the painting

shows all the money crunching – all the

desperate figuring out of how to the pay the

rent and the medical bills and the clothes for

the children – faces made prematurely old with

worry WORRY *worry*...

The painting shows the people dying in the

public hospitals for lack of medical care, the

painting shows the abandoned street children

of the Third World with nowhere to live, the

painting shows the desperation of the

shantytowns of urban Asia & Latin America &

Africa – the shantytowns of the urban Third

World rolling for miles across the treeless

landscape...

And the painting is created by people talking

on the phone, creating the painting with their

voices, the painting is launched across the

world through text messages, the painting has

a thousand languages, the painting rushes

through computers & telephones – the painting

rushes across the world in a single second to a

million different places...

The painting *dances* with poetry, the painting

mOves aroUnd a *conTemporary daNce* in

Manhattan, the painting is created on a canvas

in São Paulo Brazil, the painting walks down

the streets of Cairo, the painting rolls back-&-

forth and up-&-down with a crab boat on the

stormy Bering Sea of Alaska, the painting

soars up with the skyscrapers of Shanghai, the painting *dances* with **o**ozing-pouring-s**e**x on the streets of Trinidad with *Caribbean-sOka-rhYthms*, the painting erupts with pre-Columbian sculpture: distorted faces & gigantic torpedoing breasts & phallic tongues – the painting rushes across the sea to Japan where it plays with the sinful neighborhoods of all the major cities there – red light districts that sin up into the sky! – *the painting has a rhythm of Spanish columns dancing with the colonial architecture* throughout Latin America...

The painting *skips lightly* with the HAPPINESS of a ship crewmen after a year at sea *running joyfully* into the arms of his waiting wife & child, the painting *throbs-throbs-throbs* with the nervousness of a young man before a judge about to be sentenced for a LONG GRAY

HORRIBLE ETERNITY behind PRISON BARS for

drugs (where he will be *raped*), the painting

cries it's drops of paint with a man & wife

watching their child die because they can't

afford the medicine to keep their child alive...

www.ingramcontent.com/pod-product-compliance
Lightning Source LLC
Chambersburg PA
CBHW071215220526
45468CB00002B/615